Heart of a Hero

Heart of a Hero
CHARLES REED BISHOP

Peter Galuteria

ILLUSTRATED BY
Robin Yoko Racoma

BISHOP MUSEUM PRESS
HONOLULU, HAWAI'I

Bishop Museum is grateful to a special admirer of Charles Reed Bishop who generously supported the reprinting of Heart of a Hero: Charles Reed Bishop.

Bishop Museum Press
1525 Bernice Street
Honolulu, Hawai'i 96817
www.bishopmuseum.org/press

Copyright © 2009 by Bishop Museum

All rights reserved. No part of this book may be reproduced or transmitted in any form or by any means, electronic, mechanical, or digital including photocopying, recording, or by any information storage and retrieval system, without prior written permission from the publisher.

ISBN: 978-1-58178-094-9

Cover photo: Bradley & Rulofson, San Francisco, c. 1875. Courtesy of Bishop Museum Archives.

Design by Julie Stewart Williams
Cover design by Mardee Domingo Melton

Printed in Korea

Library of Congress Cataloging-in-Publication Data

Galuteria, Peter.
  Heart of a hero : Charles Reed Bishop / Peter Galuteria ; illustrated by Robin Yoko Racoma.
    p. cm.
  Includes bibliographical references.
  ISBN 978-1-58178-094-9 (pbk. : alk. paper) 1. Bishop, Charles Reed, 1822-1915. 2. Immigrants--Hawaii--Biography. 3. Bankers--Hawaii--Biography. 4. Philanthropists--Hawaii--Biography. 5. Hawaii--Social life and customs. 6. Hawaii--History--1893-1900--Biography. 7. Hawaii--History--1900-1959--Biography. 8. California--History--1850-1950--Biography. I. Racoma, Robin Yoko, ill. II. Title.
  DU627.17.B45G35 2009
  996.9'03092--dc22
  [B]
                              2009000928

With gratitude and aloha

I dedicate this book
to

Maria Gomes Rodrigues
my grandmother

Rose Rodrigues Galuteria
my mother

Genevieve Galuteria
my sister

Bradley Dela Cruz
my nephew

Kapualani Kauhane
my grandniece

Grant Koa Kam
my grandnephew

Brey, Douglas, Joshua, Ku'uho'ola
my great-grandnephews

Contents

Preface ix

Acknowledgments xi

Introduction 1

PART ONE
Life in New York
Early Years   1822-1846

Birth of a Hero 4

Growing Up 7

Young Man 11

Looking Westward 14

Long Voyage 16

PART TWO

Life in Hawai'i
Middle Years   1846-1894

New Land, New Friends 26

Making a Start 31

Love for a Princess 37

Marriage Made in Heaven 44

Serving and Giving 67

Serving in Business 70

Serving in Government 78

Serving in Education 83

Serving in Churches and Faith Organizations 109

Serving in Community and Other Interests 121

Live to Give 131

Leaving Hawai'i 135

PART THREE
Life in California
Later Years   1894-1915

Settling in California 140

Work and Interests 141

San Francisco Earthquake 144

Counselor, Advisor, Friend 146

Ninetieth Birthday 147

Death of a Hero 150

Royal Ceremony 151

At Rest with Pauahi 158

Greatest Benefactor 161

Conclusion 163

Bibliography..165

Preface

Here it is at last -- for the younger reader -- a biography of the Honorable Charles Reed Bishop. And how fitting! For the youth of Hawai'i are the primary beneficiaries of Mr. Bishop's enduring legacy.

Perhaps no other non-Hawaiian name is more familiar to the people of Hawai'i than that of "Bishop." He is the Bishop of such well-known places as the Bishop Bank (now called First Hawaiian Bank), Bishop Estate, Bishop Hall, Bishop Museum, Bishop Street, Bishop Trust. He is the Bishop generally remembered only as the husband of Princess Bernice Pauahi Bishop.

To this day Mr. Bishop the person remains relatively unknown. Fortunately it is now possible to fill that void by reading *Heart of a Hero: Charles Reed Bishop*. Author Peter Galuteria has diligently researched, documented and presented the life of Mr. Bishop in a meaningful way for readers of all ages.

Mr. Bishop lived a life of faith in God, hard work, caring and service to others. What better measure of the worthiness of a person's life than that of the legacy he has left behind! Through his legacy Charles Reed Bishop, Hawai'i's greatest philanthropist of the 19th century, has touched and will continue to touch the lives of numerous people today and in the many years to come.

Julie Stewart Williams

Acknowledgments

Heart of a Hero: Charles Reed Bishop represents a network of team effort. I wish to thank all who gave of their time, labor and encouragement so willingly as members of the team.

The Hawaiian studies collections of the following institutions proved invaluable:

- Bishop Museum Archives
- Hawaiʻi State Archives
- Hawaiʻi State Library
- Hawaiian Historical Society Library
- Hawaiian Mission Children's Society Library
- Kamehameha Schools Archives
- Kamehameha Schools Grades 7 and 8 Learning Center
- Kamehameha Schools Midkiff Learning Center
- Queen's Medical Center Historical Room

I commend all the staff members of these archives and libraries. Their excellent work and kind service made available many useful resources.

Now I wish to express my deep appreciation to the following people:

Robin Racoma created the captivating illustrations for the book. Her artistry reflects her sensitivity and love for the beauty of Hawai'i and its people. Her drawings enrich the meaning of the text.

Charlene Hara volunteered many hours of her own time to computerize the manuscript. She accomplished this intricate responsibility cheerfully. Her skill in computer technology helped to give the book its professional and attractive appearance.

Gussie Bento gladly gave of her time, initiative and knowledge to edit the manuscript for historical accuracy. She also helped to look through numerous photographs to select those necessary for the book. Gussie's joyful and enthusiastic manner made the work truly pleasant.

Julie Williams graciously accepted a difficult task. She edited the manuscript for clarity of meaning. She also helped to select the appropriate photographs to illustrate the biography. In addition Julie spent many hours designing the layout for the book. Her artistic skill and industrious endeavor helped to prepare the book for publication. Julie's labor of love, expertise and generosity made her contribution very special.

Thank you, team members! Your cooperation, encouragement and help have made this biography of Charles Reed Bishop available to all readers both young and old.

P.G.

Photo by B.F. Howland, San Francisco, courtesy of Bishop Museum

Charles Reed Bishop whose values, thoughts, words and deeds counted for good.

Introduction

What is a hero? A hero is a person admired for his or her outstanding qualities or achievements.

Heroes differ in shape, size and color. Some are slim. Others are stout. Some are short. Others are tall. Some are large. Others are small. Some are black or brown. Others are red, white or yellow.

However, there is one thing all heroes have in common. That one thing is a caring heart. Heroes live noble lives. They are upright in character. The values they trust count for good. The thoughts they think count for good. The words they say count for good. The deeds they do count for good. What they value, think, say and do all serve to benefit others. That is what makes them heroes.

This is the story of a hero who lived for ninety-three years. His first twenty-four years were spent in New York. His next forty-eight years were spent in Hawaiʻi. His last twenty-one years were spent in California. His was a very long life, and he lived it nobly.

This hero was a man of great vision and keen foresight. He set high goals and reached for the stars. He dreamed big dreams and fulfilled those dreams. His values, thoughts, words, deeds--all counted for good. His life was one of service, and he served many people. Truly, his heart was the heart of a hero. The name of this hero was Charles Reed Bishop.

Part One

LIFE IN NEW YORK

Early Years

1822 - 1846

Birth of a Hero

At Glens Falls, New York, a wooden toll bridge crossed the Hudson River. The middle of the bridge rested on a small island. On this island stood a tollhouse. To cross the bridge people had to pay a toll, or fee. The person who collected the fee was called the toll collector. That person at this time was Samuel Bishop. He lived in the small tollhouse with his wife Maria Reed Bishop.

Samuel and Maria were married on February 14, 1821. Then on January 25, 1822, something wonderful happened in the little tollhouse. A baby boy was born to Samuel and Maria. How happy they were! They named their son Charles Reed Bishop. The baby's cheerful sounds filled their tiny tollhouse. When he tired, the rhythmic sound of the flowing river lulled him to sleep.

Photo courtesy of Bishop Museum

The wooden toll bridge and tollhouse at Glens Falls,
New York, where Charles was born.

On May 11, 1824, Maria gave birth to another son, Henry. But two weeks after Henry's birth Maria died. How sad it was for Charles to lose his mother! And he was only two years old. When Charles was four years old tragedy struck again. This time his father Samuel Bishop died. With both parents gone Charles was now an orphan.

Growing Up

Charles was taken to his grandfather Jesse Bishop. Jesse was a hard worker. He did many kinds of work. He casted, or shaped, metals. He ran a blacksmith shop. He collected fees on a New York toll road. He managed a farm that was 123 acres in size. It was on this large farm that Charles lived with his grandfather.

Charles was baptized in a Methodist church in Glens Falls. He attended Sunday School at another Methodist church in Warrensburgh. Warrensburgh was a town just a few miles from his grandfather's home.

As a young boy Charles learned much from his grandfather. He learned the usual farm chores by caring for sheep, cattle and horses. He learned to keep the toll collector's records in good order. He learned to repair wagons, buggies and stage coaches. Like his grandfather, he became a hard worker.

Illustrated by Robin Yoko Racoma

Charles at age four with grandfather Jesse Bishop on their farm.

For his early years of education Charles attended the village school. He then spent grades seven and eight at Glens Falls Academy. His formal schooling ended when he went to work after leaving the eighth grade.

At fifteen Charles was hired by Nelson J. Warren. This man headed the largest mercantile company in Warrensburgh. His business consisted of buying and selling goods for profit. By working for him Charles learned much about business. He served as a clerk. He waited on customers. He kept the books on money. He came to know about money and its use in buying and selling goods. He also bartered, or traded goods without using money. He did the inventory. He performed maintenance tasks and janitorial duties. There was plenty to do.

Having worked all during his youth, Charles experienced much more than most boys his age. He also learned about human nature from his many relationships with other people. He became a good judge of character.

No matter what he was given to do, Charles worked hard. His willingness to work hard would remain with him for the rest of his life. He developed a deep respect for work no matter how lowly the task. He regarded honest work as something dignified and honorable. A job well done gave him a great feeling of satisfaction and joy.

Young Man

When Charles Reed Bishop was twenty years old he moved to Sandy Hill. The town of Sandy Hill was only three miles from Glens Falls. Later Sandy Hill was called Hudson Falls. Charles went to work at the Old Stone General Store. He became head clerk and bookkeeper. The store bought everything the farmers had to sell. The store also sold the farmers the supplies they needed. Charles took all of his responsibilities seriously.

There in Sandy Hill Charles met William Lee. William had just returned from college for his summer vacation. He was only a year older than Charles. The two became best of friends.

Charles stayed in Sandy Hill while William finished college. William went on to Harvard Law School. He became a lawyer. Then he moved to Troy, New York, where he opened his own office to practice law.

Meanwhile, in Sandy Hill Charles became more familiar with business. He supervised the store's post office. He became an expert in bartering. He also ran a lumber yard and a farm. He became familiar with saw mills and mills for grinding grain. He gained valuable knowledge of stage coaches, roads and communications. He came to know much more about money and its role in buying and selling. He continued to be a wise judge of character.

Charles was always careful in his work. He showed integrity, or uprightness, in all his business practices. People trusted him. They found him honest and dependable. Charles kept on working hard.

One day Charles went to Troy to visit William. The two friends were very happy to see each other again. They talked for a long time. Their discussion that day would change their lives forever.

Photo courtesy of Bishop Museum

William Lee and Charles in 1846 before sailing on the Brig Henry.

Looking Westward

What did Charles and William discuss that would change their lives so drastically? They talked about looking westward to Oregon. The Oregon Territory stretched along the northwest coast of America. It was huge. Its land contained rich soil. Its streams and rivers flowed with clear, cool water. Lush, fertile, green valleys thrived. Oregon was the land of opportunity.

The more Charles and William talked about Oregon the more excited they became. They could see so many possibilities for farming and the practice of law! They could see so many opportunities for business, commerce and industry! In all of these areas the two men were highly capable. William was a lawyer. Charles knew about farming, business and commerce. Both were excellent workers. What could be better?

With their pioneering spirit ignited, or fired up, Charles and William decided to go to Oregon. Charles would take his surveyor's compass. William would take his law books. Both would take their wisdom and experience. They were ready!

A newspaper advertisement told about a ship going to Oregon. The ship, the Brig Henry, would sail soon. Charles and William moved swiftly. They quickly booked passage on the Brig Henry. By stagecoach they hurried from Sandy Hill to Newburyport. They made the trip in three days. The ship would sail from Newburyport, Massachusetts, on February 23, 1846.

Long Voyage

A brig, or brigantine, was a sailing vessel with two masts, or tall poles rising from its deck. The masts had crosspieces called yards. Fastened to the yards were large square sails. Smaller sails were attached to the masts at the front and rear of the ship. During the 1700s and 1800s brigs served as fighting ships. They were small and fast. Brigs also served to transport cargo. Later, however, schooners and steamships replaced brigs.

The Brig Henry was small in size. Its length was 81 feet 6 inches. Its width was 20 feet 8-1/2 inches. A standard basketball court measures 94 feet long and 50 feet wide. Two Brig Henrys could fit easily within a basketball court today.

Illustrated by Robin Yoko Racoma

The Brig Henry.

The Brig Henry was scheduled to sail for Oregon. On its way it would stop in Honolulu to deliver freight. Captain William K. Kilborn, the ship's master, estimated the voyage to Oregon would take four months. The captain would be assisted by a first mate and a ship's doctor. The brig would carry sixteen passengers.

On February 23, 1846, the Brig Henry set sail. Three to four hundred spectators had gathered at the wharf to witness the brig's departure. On board were Charles Reed Bishop and William Lee. Those who came to say good-bye had tears in their eyes. They were sad to see their friends leave.

The ship left Newburyport, Massachusetts, and headed south into the Atlantic Ocean. Almost immediately rough weather set in. About midnight on February 27 Charles lay in his bunk. Suddenly a huge wave struck the ship's side. The impact threw Charles from his bunk clear over the table in his cabin. He landed about ten feet away. Stunned and dazed, he stared at his empty bunk. Bravely he managed to get back to his bunk. Fortunately, he was not hurt.

The Brig Henry in stormy seas.

This time of year was the most stormy on the Atlantic. It was cold and wet. Gales, or strong winds, tossed the small brig to and fro, as if it were straw. The bad weather slowed down the ship's progress. Charles and William had never been at sea before. How they wished they were back on dry land!

On March 15 Charles took part in the Sunday worship service. He read aloud from the *Gospel of Luke,* chapter seven, verses 11 through 17. That passage in the *Holy Bible* described how Christ brought a young lad back to life.

After eighty-four days of rough sailing, the Brig Henry reached Santa Catarina in southern Brazil. There at a port town the ship took in supplies. Charles went to the public square with two companions. He ate a lot of fruit. He took a long, pleasant stroll through the whole town. Then he returned to the ship.

No sooner had the brig left Santa Catarina when it ran into more bad weather. Every night Charles prayed with John H. Wood, a fellow passenger. They knelt in prayer at the stern, or rear, of the ship. They asked God to bless their friends and keep them safe.

Illustrated by Robin Yoko Racoma

John Wood and Charles in prayer at the ship's stern.

By the time the Henry reached the Falkland Islands, it was July 4. Captain Kilborn had said they would be in Honolulu by that date. But the bad weather had slowed them tremendously. Four months had already passed. The ship was still struggling in the Atlantic storms.

On July 16 Charles and John helped the captain. They went in the hold to look for wood and stovepipe. The hold is the space below the deck of a ship where cargo is stored. The three men worked hard. They moved many boxes and barrels. During their search they discovered a big leak. The leak, fortunately, was high above the water level and would not endanger the brig.

Ahead lay the frozen Cape Horn at the southernmost tip of South America. There the sea waters were perilous and difficult to navigate. Just off Cape Horn a severe gale hit the Henry, causing heavy damages to the ship.

Still ahead lay the vast Pacific Ocean. Days of sailing dragged into weeks. Weeks of sailing dragged into months. Although battered and bruised, the Henry sailed on and on.

Illustrated by Robin Yoko Racoma

Tracing the record breaking voyage.

At last, early in October something wonderful happened. The lofty mountain peaks of Hawai'i came into view. Sea birds flew by the ship as schools of flying fish played nearby. The brig crept closer to shore. Natives in their outrigger canoes greeted the ship. They brought bundles of fresh fruit to share with the visitors.

The Brig Henry limped into Honolulu harbor. It was leaking badly and in great need of repair. It dropped anchor on October 12, 1846. The voyage to Honolulu had taken nearly eight long months. The Brig Henry had set a record. Its voyage between New England and Hawai'i was the slowest ever!

Part Two

LIFE IN HAWAIʻI

Middle Years
1846 - 1894

New Land, New Friends

The landing place at Honolulu was shabby. The town around the port was unattractive. No one had yet dreamed of fine stone buildings rising there. Such structures would come later. Perhaps Charles and William could see the possibilities. But the young men looked beyond the port. They saw the true beauty of the place: mountains, valleys, surrounding beaches and more.

The new land was lovely. Koa trees stood tall. Kalo, or taro, grew in abundance. Fragrant maile vines sweetened the air. Flowers of many colors bloomed. Ferns and palms waved in gentle tradewinds. Fruits and vegetables tasted sweet and fresh. Puffy white clouds floated in bright blue skies. Ocean waters below reflected the magnificent color of the skies.

Photo by H.L. Chase, courtesy of Bishop Museum

Honolulu Harbor.

The air felt nice and warm. The sea felt as warm as the air. Beaches of golden sand eagerly greeted the playful, rolling surf. Almost every day the sun would shine. Nearly every night brilliant stars sparkled in the dark sky. Sometimes the sun and the stars would hide behind heavy rain clouds. And when the rains came down they filled the mountain streams. The showers brought cool water to drink and kept the landscape ever so green. To Charles and William Hawaiʻi seemed like paradise.

The people were friendly. The Hawaiians were kind and warmhearted. Their different customs delighted Charles and William. The Hawaiians welcomed the newcomers. Merchants and missionaries also made them feel at home. People in Hawaiʻi respectfully called them Mr. Bishop and Mr. Lee. Both men came to love the land and the people. In this new land they found new friends.

Illustrated by Robin Yoko Racoma

The true beauty of Hawai'i.

Mr. Bishop and Mr. Lee were supposed to go to Oregon. But now they faced a serious question. **Why not stay in Honolulu?** There was much work to do here. The growing trade could use a man like Mr. Bishop. The law office could use a man like Mr. Lee. The question called for a firm decision. Together the two men made their decision. They would stay in Honolulu.

Making a Start

Almost immediately the two young men found work. Mr. Lee took an active role as lawyer. He helped in the office of the attorney general. Then he was made superior judge. Later he became Chief Justice of the Supreme Court.

Mr. Bishop's start in Honolulu was most humble. Ladd and Company's business affairs were in bad shape. The company needed an accountant to help clear up the mess. Mr. Bishop was hired to audit, or examine, the books. By doing so he would help solve the problem and put things back in order. Later, Mr. Bishop worked as clerk for the United States Consul's office. He earned one dollar a day. But from the start he worked with endurance, honor and respect.

United States Consul's office where Mr. Bishop worked as clerk.

On February 27, 1849, Mr. Bishop became a citizen of the Hawaiian Kingdom. He promised to support its constitution and laws and to be loyal to the king. He signed an oath of allegiance. The Hawaiian Kingdom became his new native land. He was twenty-seven years old.

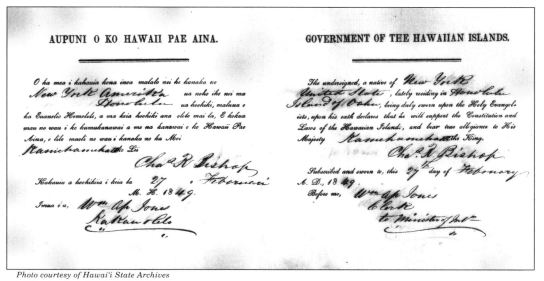

Photo courtesy of Hawai'i State Archives

Oath of allegiance in Hawaiian and English.

On March 1, 1849, Mr. Bishop was appointed to an important position. He became Collector General of Customs. He collected taxes on goods coming into the kingdom. He had the respect and admiration of many people.

Photo courtesy of Bishop Museum

Mr. Bishop became Collector General of Customs.

During his first three years in Hawai'i Mr. Bishop set a pace for himself. He balanced work with recreation and social life. He loved horseback riding. He would ride to Nuʻuanu Pali, Waikīkī and Pauoa Valley. He enjoyed informal dancing. He danced quadrilles, waltzes and polkas. He was invited to teas by Honolulu's leading families. He went to soirees, or parties given in the evening. He participated in party games such as forfeit, charades, fox and goose. He loved picnics. He visited in homes and ships with officers and crew. But what he enjoyed most was time spent with a lovely princess.

Mr. Bishop horseback riding in Waikīkī.

Love for a Princess

Princess Bernice Pauahi Pākī belonged to a high royal family. She was born on December 19, 1831. Her father was High Chief Abner Pākī. Her mother was High Chiefess Laura Konia. Her great-grandfather was King Kamehameha the Great.

Photo by H.L. Chase,
courtesy of Bishop Museum

Abner Pākī.

Photo by M. Dickson,
courtesy of Bishop Museum

Laura Konia.

The Princess was most lovely. She had attended the Royal School from childhood. It was a boarding school. She lived there. Now she was fifteen years old. Many spoke of her beauty. She was of medium height. She had graceful manners. The Princess possessed much poise. She was *"lovely in feature, form and disposition."*

Princess Pauahi was a gifted and well-rounded pupil. She was intelligent and wise. She studied many subjects in school. She played the piano and sang prettily. She painted beautiful pictures. She enjoyed horseback riding. She was the best educated of all the Hawaiian girls.

The Princess was industrious and humble. She sewed her own dresses. She knew cooking and gardening. She helped with the care of small children. She tended to the sick. She helped to clean and tidy the boarding school. She washed her own clothes. She did not complain.

The Royal School.

Princess Pauahi was kind and gentle. She showed tenderness and respect for all. Everyone thought highly of her. The Princess was very lovely on the outside. But her true beauty came from within.

Mr. Bishop, a *"dark-haired young man with a trim black beard and intense blue eyes,"* met Princess Bernice Pauahi at the Royal School. It was early in 1847. He was twenty-five years old. She was fifteen. Mr. Bishop visited often. Reading was a favorite pastime. He would read aloud to the Princess. She would play the piano and sing for him. They enjoyed each other's companionship. Mr. Bishop saw in the Princess that special kind of beauty. The Princess saw in him that special kind of gentleman.

Illustrated by Robin Yoko Racoma

Reading was a favorite pastime for Mr. Bishop and Princess Pauahi.

Love began to grow between Mr. Bishop and Princess Pauahi. The months went by. More than two years passed. The couple fell deeply in love. They wished to be married.

Marriage would not come easily. Pauahi's parents, Pākī and Konia, opposed the idea. They did not want their daughter to marry a foreigner. They had hoped she would marry a prince. Then she would someday become queen. The Princess loved her parents. She did not wish to hurt them. But she felt she must marry the man she loved.

Princess Pauahi and Mr. Bishop would not give up. They loved each other dearly. Their love was a *"match made in heaven."* Despite the opposition they decided to go forward with marriage.

Photo by [Senor Le Bleu?],
courtesy of Bishop Museum

Princess Pauahi at age 15.

Photo courtesy of
Bishop Museum

Mr. Bishop at age 24.

Marriage Made in Heaven

The Wedding and Honeymoon

The wedding of Mr. Bishop and Princess Pauahi was simple. It took place the evening of June 4, 1850, in the Royal School parlor. Mr. Bishop was twenty-eight years old. The Princess was eighteen. The beautiful young bride wore a gown of white muslin. On her head was a lei of pīkake, or jasmine. Few people were present. The parents of the bride did not attend. They still opposed the marriage. After the quick ceremony, tea was served. The whole affair took one hour, from eight to nine o'clock.

The next day Mr. and Mrs. Bishop left on their honeymoon. They sailed for Kōloa, Kaua'i. Their honeymoon lasted three weeks.

Photo courtesy of Bishop Museum

Wedding picture of Mr. and Mrs. Charles Reed Bishop, 1850.

Humble Beginning

On July 2 the Bishops returned to Honolulu. They stayed in the home of Judge Lorrin Andrews. Later they moved to a cottage the judge owned in Nuʻuanu Valley. They would live there while their new home was being built.

Mr. Bishop had purchased a piece of property. It was at the northeast corner of Hotel and Alakea Streets. This is where their new home would stand.

The Bishops soon moved into their new home. It was small and very modest. Mr. Bishop had not yet earned his great wealth. But in four short years in Hawaiʻi he had saved enough cash. With it he bought the land. Now he provided a cottage for his bride. This spoke well for his diligence and thrift.

Mr. and Mrs. Bishop were thrilled to be in their own home. The bride practiced all she had learned about homemaking. She made their home a pleasant place to live. How happy they were!

Mr. Bishop.

Mrs. Bishop.

Photos courtesy of Bishop Museum

Their new home - a small cottage.

Family Harmony

One day Mrs. Bishop got a big surprise. Her father Pākī came to visit. She had not seen her father since before the wedding. And that meeting had been somewhat trying. Mrs. Bishop was so happy to see her father again. He seemed to fill the small living room with his size. Pākī was six feet four inches tall. He weighed about three hundred pounds. He possessed great strength. Yet he humbled himself to visit his daughter. This marked an attempt to restore family harmony.

After Pākī left, he sent Pauahi a gift. It was a huge ornamental mirror. It was placed in the front room. There was hardly any space for it. From the floor the mirror reached the ceiling. The size of it showed how much Pākī loved his daughter.

Photos courtesy of Bishop Museum

Mrs. Bishop at age 23.   Mr. Bishop at age 33.

In time Konia and Pākī accepted the marriage fully. They saw how truly happy the couple were. They really came to know their son-in-law Mr. Bishop. They found him to be industrious and honest. They saw him accepted into the highest circles of society. They saw how wise and kind he was. They saw how deeply he loved their daughter. They saw how greatly he cared for her. Mr. and Mrs. Bishop were thankful. Harmony with her parents was now complete. Their marriage was off to a wonderful start.

Inheritance

A few years later on June 13, 1855, Pākī died. He left to his daughter everything he owned. He gave her 5,780 acres of land on Oʻahu. He also gave her Haleakalā, his new home.

From W.T. Brigham Collection, courtesy of Bishop Museum

Haleakalā built by Pākī and left to Pauahi in 1855.
Mr. Bishop seated on porch.

Haleakalā was a magnificent house. It was a large two-story stone-and-frame building. On three sides of the house were lānai, or porches. Tall pillars on both floors supported the lānai. Haleakalā was built where Pākī's old house once stood. The beautiful gardens of Haleakalā combined plants, flowers and trees. A special tamarind tree grew near the house. It had been planted at Pauahi's birth. The property was bordered by the present Fort, Hotel, Bishop and King Streets.

Mr. and Mrs. Bishop moved into Haleakalā. They lived with Konia, Pauahi's mother, and Lili'u, Pauahi's hānai sister. Lili'u later ruled as Queen Lili'uokalani. Also staying on the property were many helpers. They lived in thatched houses surrounding the big house. They loved the Bishops.

On July 2, 1857, Konia died, just two years after Pākī. She left to her daughter Pauahi about 11,560 acres of land. Mrs. Bishop's estate was growing.

Ambrotype by W.F. Howland, courtesy of Bishop Museum

Pauahi and her hānai sister, Liliʻu.

Hospitality

The Bishops were the most gracious host and hostess. Their home became the center of hospitality in Honolulu. The Bishops always made time for others.

People from many countries came to visit the Bishops. They enjoyed tea parties. They played games of tennis or croquet. They took part in evening dances.

The Bishops welcomed many Honolulu people to their home. The women of the sewing society from church met there. Their husbands would later join them for supper. The Stranger's Friend Society held meetings at Haleakalā. This organization helped people stranded in Honolulu without money or friends. Some evenings small groups gathered for reading, conversation, or music.

Mrs. Bishop also found time to teach piano lessons. Sometimes she invited her pupils to stay for lunch. They just loved it when this took place.

Mrs. Bishop at age 35.

Photos by B.F. Howland, San Francisco, courtesy of Bishop Museum

Mr. Bishop at age 45.

People came for counseling. Mrs. Bishop would spend hours talking with them. She listened to their needs, often beneath her tamarind tree. With her young friends Mrs. Bishop shared these words:

> *"Young ladies, your life is before you—it will be what you choose to make it. Times will come when you will feel you are being pushed into the background. Never allow this to happen—stand always on your own foundation. But you will have to make that foundation. There will come times when to make this stand will be difficult, especially to you of Hawaiian birth; but conquer you can—if you will."*

Mr. Bishop always supported the kind deeds of his wife. People called her, *"The lady who walks in the sunshine."* Both Mr. and Mrs. Bishop tried to bring sunshine to someone's life every day.

Throughout their married life the Bishops were known for hospitality. At home their days were busy and happy. Everyone loved them dearly.

Prosperity

Through the years Mrs. Bishop inherited many acres of land. Both of her parents left her their lands. Later she would inherit 353,000 acres of Kamehameha lands from her cousin, Princess Ruth Keʻelikōlani. Princess Ruth also left Pauahi her huge mansion, Keōua Hale. Mrs. Bishop would own the largest estate in Hawaiʻi.

As the years went by, Mr. Bishop proved to be very successful in everything he did. He became wealthy on his own. His knowledge, skills, and determination made him one of the richest men in all Hawaiʻi.

The Bishops became very prosperous, or successful and wealthy. But how does one measure prosperity? True prosperity goes deeper than money. True prosperity is measured by one's character. People who are truly prosperous keep well-rounded lives. They set good examples of balanced living. Mr. and Mrs. Bishop were excellent examples.

Photo by Ray Jerome Baker, courtesy of Bishop Museum

Keōua Hale, Princess Ruth's mansion left to Pauahi.

The Bishops lived their life in proper balance. They kept their **mind** alert. Together they read books and discussed many interesting topics.

The Bishops kept their **body** healthy. Together they walked, played, danced and did horseback riding.

The Bishops kept their **spirit** alive. Together they prayed and went to church to worship God. They taught Sunday School.

The Bishops kept their **emotions** stable. Together they were at peace with themselves and with everyone. They had great love for all people.

The Bishops kept their **social life** active. Together they graciously opened their home to many. They spent much time with people from all walks of life.

The Bishops were not blessed with children of their own. Yet in a sense their lives touched every child. Their time, energy and gifts became a blessing to many children.

The Bishops shared their prosperity with the children of Hawai'i. Mrs. Bishop would leave her estate for education. The Kamehameha Schools are the result. Mr. Bishop would give freely of his wealth. He helped many boys and girls. This resulted in greatly improved lives. The Bishops loved all children.

Mrs. Bishop at age 40.
Photo by W. Kurtz, New York,
courtesy of Bishop Museum

Mr. Bishop at age 50.
Photo courtesy of Bishop Museum

Travel

After many years of busy life, the Bishops took time to travel. Mr. Bishop had worked hard. He experienced success. Now husband and wife were ready to see the world.

Where did their travel take them? The Bishops first visited California. Then in 1871 they toured northeast United States. They visited Glens Falls and Sandy Hill in New York. Here was where Mr. Bishop had spent his boyhood. Then off to Maine the Bishops went. While on a picnic they met an Indian chief. The chief mistook Mrs. Bishop for an American Indian. He asked to what tribe she belonged. Mrs. Bishop spoke briefly to him in Hawaiian. Then in English she explained that she came from the Hawaiian Kingdom. She shared what her country was like. The chief was fascinated.

In 1875 the Bishops traveled to Europe. That year marked their silver wedding anniversary. They had been married for twenty-five years.

In Europe the Bishops visited many countries. They toured Ireland, Scotland, England, Germany, Austria, France, Italy and Monaco. They had only read about these places in books. Now they were there in person.

In Rome the Bishops were presented to Pope Pius IX. In London they met Queen Victoria. Wherever they went the Bishops were received well. They enjoyed their travel. They saw and did so much.

Photos courtesy of Bishop Museum

Mrs. Bishop, age 43. Mr. Bishop, age 53.
In Italy on December 9, 1875.

Mr. and Mrs. Bishop in San Francisco, 1876.

Closing Years of Marriage

The Bishops returned from their travel. Back to their joyful commitments they went. Several years passed. They kept as busy as ever.

Then one day tragedy struck. Mrs. Bishop's health weakened. She became seriously ill with cancer. She suffered patiently for several months. On October 16, 1884, Mrs. Bishop died. She was fifty-two years of age. At her bedside was her husband, Mr. Bishop. He was overwhelmed with grief. How greatly he would miss his beloved wife!

Mrs. Bishop was buried with all the honors due a high chiefess. She was laid to rest at Mauna'ala, the Royal Mausoleum.

Mr. and Mrs. Bishop were married for over thirty-four years. They loved each other deeply. No one can truly describe the depth of that love.

Mrs. Bishop, who died on October 16, 1884.

Serving and Giving

Through the years Mr. Bishop served faithfully. He served in business. He served in government. He served in education. He served in churches. He served in community interests.

Serving became a way of life for Mr. Bishop. He aimed to serve. He practiced it. He endured in it. He never tired of serving others. This was always his primary concern. Mr. Bishop served in the way the following poem urges:

> *"Be not weary in your serving;*
> *Do your best for those in need;*
> *Kindnesses will be rewarded*
> *By the Lord, Who prompts the deed."*
> *–Anonymous*

Giving was also important to Mr. Bishop. He became a great benefactor, or one who gives freely.

How did Mr. Bishop learn to give? He learned by example. He read about George Peabody. This man lived first in America and then in England. He was very rich. Like Mr. Bishop he was born poor. He left school at the end of eighth grade. He worked hard for his money. Mr. Peabody had his own plan of giving. He gave money away for good purposes. He gave while he was still living. He did not wait to leave it in a Will. He wanted to see how his money was helping others. This made him happy.

Mr. Bishop's **mind** to give was inspired by the giving plan of George Peabody. But Mr. Bishop's **heart** to give was moved by the generous nature of the Hawaiian people. Still, whatever he learned to do, he learned by actually doing it. He learned to give by giving. Mr. Bishop gave money away for good purposes. He gave money away while he was still living. By doing so he could see how his money helped others. This made him happy.

At first giving money away was not easy for Mr. Bishop. But he kept at it. He gave bit by bit. Gradually, he gave more and more. His giving was done with a cheerful spirit. As a result, giving became his way of living.

Photo by Bradley & Rulofson, San Francisco, courtesy of Bishop Museum

Mr. Bishop never tired of serving and giving.

Serving in Business

Līhuʻe Plantation, 1849

Mr. Bishop was one of the first three supporters of the Līhuʻe Plantation. He invested $4,000 which was one-fourth of the total first investment. Līhuʻe Plantation played a key role in raising sugar cane in Hawaiʻi.

Aldrich and Bishop General Store, 1853

William A. Aldrich and Mr. Bishop became partners in business. They opened the Aldrich and Bishop General Store. The store sold a variety of goods. It was located in the first three-story brick building in Honolulu. This building had just been completed in time for the store's opening.

Mr. Bishop invested in Līhu'e Plantation.

Aldrich and Bishop General Store located in far left of the building.

Bishop and Company, 1858

Mr. Bishop saw the need for a bank. So he and Mr. Aldrich opened Hawaiʻi's first bank. It was named Bishop and Company. Its purpose was to provide general banking business. Also included was a savings bank. The two men worked as clerk, cashier, bookkeeper and janitor. The bank did well from the start. Bishop and Company was the third largest bank west of the Rocky Mountains.

Following 1876 certain businesses in Hawaiʻi were in great financial trouble. They needed help from the bank. Mr. Bishop's bank came to the rescue. He took on the money matters until the danger passed. Mr. Bishop's kindness, integrity and care became the model of his bank.

Through the years the bank grew. It took on many changes. One of the changes was its name. The name Bishop and Company changed to Bishop Bank. Then in 1969 it became the First Hawaiian Bank.

Bishop and Company.

Photos courtesy of Bishop Museum

Bishop Bank.

Photo by Daniel Georgia

First Hawaiian Bank Building
(First Hawaiian Center)
dedicated on October 18, 1996.

Hōnaunau (South Kona, Hawai'i), 1867

Mr. Bishop purchased 7,120 acres of land in Hōnaunau. This was good coffee and grazing land. In 1891 Mr. Bishop gave this land to the Bernice Pauahi Bishop Estate. It would benefit The Kamehameha Schools.

Moloka'i Property, 1875

Mr. Bishop owned 46,500 acres of ranch land on Moloka'i. In 1893 he gave all his Moloka'i property to the Bernice Pauahi Bishop Estate. The property would benefit The Kamehameha Schools.

Waipi'o Valley (Island of Hawai'i), 1881

Mr. Bishop acquired Waipi'o Valley in 1881. In 1892 he deeded Waipi'o to the Bernice Pauahi Bishop Estate Trustees. They were to manage Waipi'o Valley. Income from the property was to benefit the Bernice Pauahi Bishop Museum.

In 1896 Mr. Bishop established the Bernice Pauahi Bishop Museum Trust. A trust is property or money held and managed by one person or group for the benefit of another. As a result, Waipiʻo Valley was deeded to the newly established Bishop Museum Trust. Now the Bishop Museum Trustees would manage the property to benefit the Museum.

Photo courtesy of Bishop Museum

Waipiʻo Valley (Island of Hawaiʻi) acquired by Mr. Bishop in 1881.

Serving in Government

Served Six Rulers, 1849-1893

Mr. Bishop lived in Hawai'i during the reigns of six monarchs. Kauikeaouli (Kamehameha III) ruled from 1825 to 1854. Alexander Liholiho (Kamehameha IV) ruled from 1854 to 1863. Lot Kamehameha (Kamehameha V) ruled from 1863 to 1872.

Kamehameha III.

Kamehameha IV.

Kamehameha V.

William Charles Lunalilo ruled from 1873 to 1874. David Kalākaua ruled from 1874 to 1891. Queen Liliʻuokalani ruled from 1891 to 1893.

Lunalilo.

Kalākaua.

Liliʻuokalani.

Photos courtesy of Bishop Museum

Mr. Bishop was a friend of all six rulers. He served the six rulers well. He became advisor to the last five monarchs.

Collector General of Customs, 1849-1853

Mr. Bishop served as Collector General of Customs. He was also appointed to the Customs Commission. This board was given authority to make rules about goods entering Hawai'i. It also heard appeals, or requests, and made decisions on those appeals. Mr. Bishop did his work faithfully and well. The Privy Council and King Kamehameha III were thankful for his work.

Member Privy Council, 1859-1892

The Privy Council was a very powerful body in Hawaiian government. It was made up of the heads of five main departments all appointed by the King. They were Interior, Foreign Affairs, Finance, Public Instruction and Attorney General. Also included were the governors of the four main islands. In addition the King appointed a few other members as well. The Privy Council was the executive branch of government. It was responsible for advising the King. The Council helped the King manage the government.

Mr. Bishop was appointed to the Privy Council in 1859. He served for thirty-three years. His attendance record was the best of any member. In his role as councilor he kept the rulers on a steady course.

Member House of Nobles, 1859-1892

The House of Nobles was the legislative branch of government. It was responsible for making laws. Mr. Bishop served in several ways at different times. He headed the Finance Committee. He chaired the Foreign Relations Committee. He helped on the Commerce and Manufacturing Committee. He headed the Foreign Affairs Committee. He chaired the Education Committee. He was elected President of the full assembly twice. Mr. Bishop served for thirty-three years in the House of Nobles.

Foreign Minister Under King Lunalilo, 1873

Mr. Bishop served as Foreign Minister during King Lunalilo's reign. He had many responsibilities. Mr. Bishop was involved in all important matters of Hawaiian government. Most of his letters in any one year period were written during this time. His devotion to King Lunalilo was genuine. He was highly trusted by the King. He served well as Foreign Minister.

Honors and Awards

Mr. Bishop received many honors and awards for his service. Included were crosses, stars, cordons, ribbons, medals and pendants. From Emperor Meiji of Japan he received the Imperial First Order of the Rising Sun. This honor was given to Mr. Bishop for his respect in labor trade. It was the highest honor Japan could give a foreigner. Today the collection of honors and awards can be seen at the Bernice Pauahi Bishop Museum.

Serving in Education

Public Education. Board Member, 1869-1883, 1887-1894.

Mr. Bishop took a keen interest in education. He was a member of the Board of Education for twenty-one years. He served as President of the Board of Education under Lunalilo, Kalākaua and Liliʻuokalani. He held this position under the Monarchy, the Provisional Government, and the Republic. As such he influenced the growth of public education in Hawaiʻi. Schools were built. Modern ways of teaching were tried. Hawaiians became the most educated island people in the world.

The Kamehameha Schools.
Trustee, 1884-1897.

In her Will, Mrs. Bishop had set up a trust. Her Estate would create and support The Kamehameha Schools. She wanted a School for Boys and a School for Girls. Character building and preparation for earning a living were important to her. These were the objectives the Founder of the Schools had in mind. She knew the advantages of education. Success would depend upon moral character, intelligence and industry.

Mrs. Bishop had named five trustees to carry out her trust. She named her husband first. So Mr. Bishop served on the first Board of Trustees for the Bernice Pauahi Bishop Estate.

Mr. Bishop knew the value of land. He emphasized that the Estate lands should not be sold. In time the Estate would grow in value. Mr. Bishop knew this would happen. Thus he advised against selling the Estate lands. Moreover, this policy was in keeping with Pauahi's Will and her great love and respect for the land.

Portrait by Norman D. Hill, courtesy of Bishop Museum

Kamehameha I for whom The Kamehameha Schools were named.

Photo by Williams, courtesy of Bishop Museum

Mr. Bishop named by Mrs. Bishop as the first Trustee for the Bernice Pauahi Bishop Estate.

Mr. Bishop's greatest service in education was for The Kamehameha Schools. He knew exactly what Mrs. Bishop wanted and why. He saw to it that the wish of his dear wife was carried out. He had the skills and means to do it. He played a key role in establishing The Kamehameha Schools.

The Kamehameha Schools campus was located where the Bishop Museum stands today. It also included the area occupied now by Farrington High School and Kamehameha Housing.

In the early years money was not always available. Yet money was needed for constructing the necessary school buildings. So during those years Mr. Bishop came to the rescue. To establish The Kamehameha Schools he gave much of his personal funds.

With his own money Mr. Bishop built Bishop Hall to start the School for Boys. Bishop Hall was the first classroom building. The School for Boys was officially opened on November 4, 1887.

Photo courtesy of Hawai'i State Archives

Bishop Hall, first classroom building for
The Kamehameha School for Boys.

On December 19, 1887, Mr. Bishop gave the first Founder's Day address. It was in honor of his wife the Founder who was born on December 19, 1831. When Mr. Bishop entered the Hall he was greeted by singing. The voices rang out with joyful song. Mr. Bishop's presence pleased everyone. The audience was made up of the select student body. Also present were Hawaiian royalty and fellow townspeople. In his message Mr. Bishop expressed the Founder's wish. He shared how she loved her people. He emphasized that the Schools are to be permanent. They are to improve in method as time goes on. They are intended for capable, industrious and well-behaved youths.

The Preparatory Department followed. It was opened on October 29, 1888, and dedicated on Founder's Day, December 19, the same year.

Finally came the School for Girls. Mr. Bishop built the first building for the Girls' School. The opening celebration took place on December 19, 1894.

Three years later Mr. Bishop built the Bernice Pauahi Bishop Memorial Chapel in memory of his wife. It was dedicated on December 19, 1897.

Photo courtesy of Hawai'i State Archives

School for Boys Chorus performing on a special occasion.

Mr. Bishop wanted to know every student in the Schools. He wished to be able to call each one by name. He would always take an interest in the welfare and success of every student. At Christmas he remembered the students with gifts. One Christmas he gave them bats and balls. The students were so happy. In no time they were outside playing ball.

Through the years Mr. Bishop emphasized the value of character first, the value of health second and the value of learning and success third. He saw these values as being very necessary for the Schools.

First, Mr. Bishop pointed out that the moral character of all connected with the Schools is of the greatest importance. He stressed that a person's character and reputation are very precious. Therefore, self-control and discipline are to be taught. Second, proper exercise, balanced meals and adequate rest are essential for good health. Also, neatness and cleanliness are to be promoted. Third, students are to value educational opportunities and make the most of them. They are to put into practice the sound principles they have learned. Only then will they become successful persons.

Photo by Frank Davey, courtesy of Bishop Museum

Main Hall of the School for Girls.

Photo courtesy of Hawai'i State Archives

Kamehameha students on Founder's Day at Mauna'ala.

Mr. Bishop wanted the Schools to show goodness and kindness among the staff and students. The friendships formed at the Schools should be lasting. This would motivate the graduates to be helpful to each other and to the Schools all their lives. Mr. Bishop emphasized the need for *"a Christian teacher who will take an interest in and help in the moral training of the boys [and girls]."*

Mr. Bishop wanted those students who did well in their school work to be trained as teachers. He felt **teaching** to be the most useful work. Through the use of their knowledge and **good character**, teachers could exert a positive influence on their students.

The Preparatory Department was Mr. Bishop's special contribution to Kamehameha. He saw many younger Hawaiian boys with no home or school. His wife's Will did not include a school for younger children. So Mr. Bishop offered to build one for them. He would pay for this school with his own money. It would become a department of The Kamehameha Schools. The Trustees gratefully approved and accepted his generous offer and gift.

Photo by Ray Jerome Baker, courtesy of Bishop Museum

Students are to value educational opportunities.

The Preparatory Department began as a boarding school for young Hawaiian boys. Boys between the ages of seven and twelve years were enrolled. They were well cared for. They were taught good morals and manners. Cleanliness and neatness were stressed. Instruction was given in English, numbers, drawing, penmanship and singing. The course of study prepared the youngsters to enter the higher Schools.

Mr. Bishop helped establish The Kamehameha Schools on a firm foundation. The School for Boys, the School for Girls and the Preparatory Department were now all in place. Through the years the Schools have educated many Hawaiian boys and girls. Mr. Bishop's service to The Kamehameha Schools has been felt to this day.

Punahou School (Oʻahu College). Trustee, 1867-1897.

Punahou School was very special to Mr. Bishop. He first got to know the School through sports. He often spent Saturday afternoons on the Punahou campus. He went there to play *"bat and ball"* with the students. His interest in the School grew. Years later in 1867 he became a Punahou Trustee.

Young Hawaiian boys at the Preparatory Department boarding school.

Photo by Alonzo Gartley, courtesy of Bishop Museum

Bishop Hall of Science, Punahou School.

Mr. Bishop served as Trustee for thirty years. His record of attending the meetings was outstanding. He served on many committees. These included education, insurance, land purchase, penmanship. He also worked on the committee to study the establishment of a primary school.

Mr. Bishop urged that Punahou be made the best kind of school. It should be *"vigorous and thorough in all that it undertakes…high in moral tone, high in the quality of all its instruction, and high in its elevating and refining influences."* Punahou School *"should try to be the leader in the contest against vice and ignorance."* These words of Mr. Bishop apply even today.

Photo by H.F. Hill, courtesy of Bishop Museum

Pauahi Hall, Punahou School.

Mr. Bishop emphasized the importance of physical training. In addition he stressed the need for excellence in education. In his own words:

> *"Physical training should receive more attention at Punahou, especially with the girls. It can be made beneficial, graceful and attractive. With a larger endowment, great care in selection of teachers, a liberal supply of apparatus, vigilance and considerable sacrifice of time by the trustees, and helpful interest of parents and guardians, the College [Punahou] can be made so excellent and attractive that the best teachers and the scholars will be proud to be connected with it. It is mainly the teachers, of whom the president is the most important, that make the character of the school, and they need and should have all the support that can be given them."*

Photo by Elias Shura, courtesy of Bishop Museum

Charles Reed Bishop Hall, Punahou School.

Through the years Mr. Bishop donated much to Punahou. As a result scholarships were made available. Students who had little or no money could attend Punahou. In addition buildings were erected: Bishop Hall of Science, Pauahi Hall and Charles Reed Bishop Hall. These all came about as a result of his gifts. Also, a collection of precious oil paintings was given to Punahou by Mr. Bishop.

January 25, 1915, marked Mr. Bishop's ninety-third birthday. On that day the students of Punahou gathered to celebrate his life and works. President Arthur Floyd Griffiths spoke these words:

> *"I cannot let this occasion pass without reminding the students of the great debt that Punahou has to Mr. Bishop. He has given generously in money...He has given freely of himself. Although he is not a graduate of Punahou no one has had more interest in its welfare and advancement. His services as trustee were marked by the greatest devotion to the advancement of the interests of the school."*

Bernice Pauahi Bishop Museum.
Founded in 1889.

In 1889 Mr. Bishop founded the Bernice Pauahi Bishop Museum in memory of his beloved wife. He remembered Pauahi's dream of a special place. She had dreamed of a place where precious heirlooms and other beautiful things could be preserved and displayed for people to see. During their travels to America and Europe, the Bishops had visited many museums. Hawai'i had no such place.

Mr. Bishop paid for the planning and construction of the first buildings. He provided valuable leadership and guidance during the early years of the Museum. In 1896 he set up the Bernice Pauahi Bishop Museum Trust which would help to support the Museum and its work.

Through the years, the Museum has increased greatly in size and scope. There are more departments, exhibit halls, offices, storerooms and workrooms. There are shops, a library and an archives. A planetarium and an observatory have been added. Native flora can be seen growing throughout the grounds.

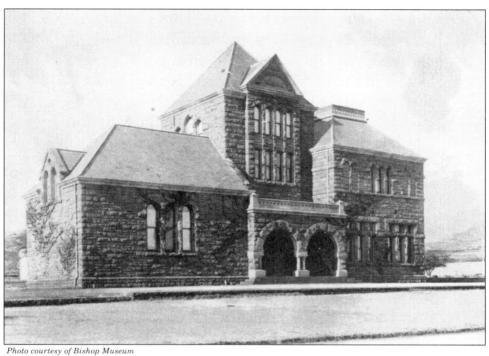
Photo courtesy of Bishop Museum

Hawaiʻi Hall, Bernice Pauahi Bishop Museum.

The collections, exhibits and educational programs are many. They cover primarily the natural environment and the cultural and social history of the vast Pacific region. A huge variety of specimens have been collected, preserved, stored, studied and exhibited. For example, the Museum now has the world's largest collection of Micronesian land shells. It also has the world's largest single collection of Hawaiian feather capes and cloaks.

The work of the Museum is based upon extensive scientific research. The staff consists of people who are highly educated and with many years of experience. They are noted experts in their fields of study. The Museum publishes significant research studies as well as books written by authorities in their subject.

The Museum seeks to share its resources and to educate people. During World War II, for instance, America faced a unique problem. It needed to train men to survive under difficult experiences. What should one do when cast adrift in the ocean? How can one survive if stranded on a lonely Pacific island? The Museum was glad to provide survival training courses for the Army. Life-saving skills were taught to 150,000 men.

Photo courtesy of Bishop Museum

Interior of Hawai'i Hall.

This world-renowned Museum is a vital educational center. It has kept pace with modern technology as well as current issues. It invites the public to participate in its community events, demonstrations and hands-on activities. Many of its activities are created especially for children.

The Bishop Museum is a place where Hawaiʻi's residents and visitors from all over the world can come. They can come to satisfy their curiosity or to do research. They can come to learn something new or simply to relax and enjoy. All of this is possible today because of Mr. Bishop's generosity, his deep love for his wife, Bernice Pauahi Bishop, and his desire to fulfill her dream.

Honolulu Library and Reading Room Association. President, 1892-1906.

Mr. Bishop was always fond of books. He wrote, *"Books really worth reading are good companions."* So it was natural for him to join the Honolulu Library and Reading Room Association. He served as its President for several years. He gave of his efforts and money to its support. This association became the Library of Hawai'i.

Other Schools

Mr. Bishop served other private schools with his time or money. The schools were Mills Institute, Kawaiaha'o Seminary, Makawao Female Seminary, Kohala Girls' School, Waialua Female Seminary and Hilo Boys' Boarding School. Most of these schools no longer exist. However, in 1907 Mills Institute and Kawaiaha'o Seminary banded together. They became Mid-Pacific Institute as it is known today.

Photo by Montano, courtesy of Bishop Museum

Mr. Bishop served many schools.

Serving in Churches and Faith Organizations

Moral and spiritual values were important to Mr. Bishop. That is why he took steps to serve in ways that he could. He participated in churches and other faith organizations.

Kaumakapili Church and Kawaiahaʻo Church

Kaumakapili Church and Kawaiahaʻo Church captured Mr. Bishop's concern. Both churches consisted largely of Hawaiian members. Mr. Bishop gladly gave them his support.

Photo courtesy of Hawai'i State Archives

The first Kaumakapili Church, dedicated in 1839, stood at Smith and Beretania Streets on land given by Pākī and Konia.

Photo by L.E. Edgeworth, courtesy of Bishop Museum

The third Kaumakapili Church, dedicated in 1911, stands at its present site on North King Street.

The second Kaumakapili Church, dedicated in 1888,
replaced the first church at Smith and Beretania Streets.

Photo courtesy of Bishop Museum

Kawaiahaʻo Church received Mr. Bishop's support.
Mrs. Bishop taught Sunday School at Kawaiahaʻo Church.

Bethel Union Church and Fort Street Church

Mr. Bishop taught a Sunday School class at Bethel Union Church. He taught there in the first years of his marriage. For morning service his wife always went to Kawaiahaʻo Church. Mrs. Bishop was a member and taught Sunday School there. But in the evening Mr. and Mrs. Bishop would worship together. They attended evening service at Fort Street Church regularly.

Bethel Union had started Fort Street Church. Thus Bethel Union was the mother church. Fort Street Church was the daughter church. Soon they would merge, or band together, as one.

Central Union Church

In 1887 Bethel Union and Fort Street Church merged to form Central Union Church. Mr. Bishop served on the merger committee. He had been a faithful visitor at Fort Street Church for thirty-five years. Now he offered his services to the new church.

Photo courtesy of Bishop Museum

Bethel Union Church at King and Bethel Streets in Honolulu.

Photo courtesy of Bishop Museum

Fort Street Church at Fort and Beretania Streets in Honolulu.

The first meeting of Central Union Church Board was held in Mr. Bishop's home. Mr. Bishop was elected President of the Board of Trustees. He used his skills to help Central Union Church. He helped in counsel, in construction and in business problems. He supervised the construction of the building. He saw to the planning and the making of the stained glass windows. He served as a faithful Trustee of Central Union Church for several years.

Central Union Church at Beretania and Richards Streets in Honolulu.

Bernice Pauahi Bishop Memorial Chapel

Mr. Bishop saw the need for a Chapel for Kamehameha Schools. He decided to build one in memory of his dear wife. He would name it the Bernice Pauahi Bishop Memorial Chapel. Mr. Bishop spent much time on the plans and details. He was wise. He would sit down to count the cost. Then he made the best choice and took the right steps.

The building was completed in 1897. Mr. Bishop received great joy. The Chapel would be an important gift to the spiritual training of Kamehameha students. Mr. Bishop wrote these words:

> *"The appearance of the Chapel is much praised, and I hope that the service in it will always be attractive, elevating, and helpful toward right living, so that it may be a blessing and delight to all who are or may be connected with the Schools. It is intended for a place of worship, and I believe that the worship most acceptable to you is, such as is taught in the life and words of Jesus and as awakens and strengthens love for and helpfulness to mankind."*

Bernice Pauahi Bishop Memorial Chapel.
Located where Farrington High School Auditorium stands today.

Faith Organizations

Through the years Mr. Bishop served freely. He participated in the efforts of the following faith groups.

American Relief Fund Association

Hawaiian Bible Society

Hawaiian Evangelical Association

Hawaiian Mission Children's Society

Hawaiian Missionary Society

Hawaiian Temperance Society

Sailors' Home of Honolulu

Young Men's Christian Association

Through these various groups Mr. Bishop helped to serve. He always showed love and interest in the welfare of others.

Serving in Community and Other Interests

Kalaupapa, Moloka'i

Mr. Bishop showed great concern over the health needs of Hawai'i. The Hawaiian Kingdom was hit by various diseases. These diseases included measles, small pox, cholera and leprosy. Sometimes they occurred on a large scale, known as epidemics. The disease that caused Mr. Bishop the greatest concern was leprosy.

Leprosy, or Hansen's disease, is spread from one person to another by germs or viruses. The disease attacks the skin and nerves. It weakens the muscles. It causes lumps, spots and open sores. If not treated, the injury to the nerves results in numbness, paralysis and deformity.

Photo courtesy of Bishop Museum

Kalaupapa, Molokaʻi.

Efforts were made by the Hawaiian government to stop the spread of leprosy. This was done by isolating, or setting apart, those with the disease. They were sent to Kalaupapa, Moloka'i. The place was surrounded by sheer cliffs and deep ocean.

Mr. Bishop took necessary steps to help the patients there. Several single women and girls had no guardians or caregivers. They were in need of a home and nurses to care for them. Mr. Bishop generously provided the Bishop Home for Girls. It consisted of a dormitory for girls and a cottage for their caregivers and guardians. It also had a dining house, kitchen, recreation hall, bath house and toilets. The group of houses had some fencing with gates and turnstiles.

Mr. Bishop's generous offer of the Home for Girls made it possible for several nurses to help at Kalaupapa. These nurses were sisters, or nuns, of the Roman Catholic Church. They were supervised by Sister Marianne, Mother Superior of the Franciscan Sisters. They became the guardians and caregivers for the young women and girls. Later Mr. Bishop provided a chapel for the Bishop Home for Girls at Kalaupapa.

Bishop Home for Girls at Kalaupapa.

Bishop Chapel at Kalaupapa.

In 1896 Mother Marianne wrote:

> *"... I am sure if he [Mr. Bishop] knew how many poor girls he has saved from immorality he would feel more than happy for having founded this, 'Home'. God bless him."*

Queen's Hospital

Mr. Bishop showed keen interest in Queen's Hospital from its start. King Kamehameha IV and Queen Emma, Founders of Queen's, personally had been seeking donations to begin the hospital. Mr. and Mrs. Bishop were among the very first donors.

Through the years Mr. Bishop became a leading benefactor of Queen's Hospital. Funds he gave made possible the building of the Pauahi Wing for the hospital. The first Pauahi Wing was completed in 1905.

Mr. Bishop willingly shared his leadership skills with Queen's Hospital. He served as Trustee for thirty-six years from 1859 to 1895. He also served as Treasurer from 1859 to 1873. In addition he was Vice President from 1880 to 1894. Queen's is today one of the leading medical centers of the Pacific region.

First Pauahi Wing at Queen's Hospital completed in 1905.

Mr. Bishop showed concern for other hospitals as well. These included Kauikeōlani Children's Hospital, Kapiʻolani Maternity Home and Lēʻahi Hospital.

Royal Hawaiian Agricultural Society

Mr. Bishop was one of three Founders of the Royal Hawaiian Agricultural Society. He served as Secretary and Treasurer. The society was interested in agriculture in Hawaiʻi. Its members were progressive, energetic men.

Hawaiian Historical Society

The Hawaiian Historical Society sought to study, preserve and use historical material. The society was interested in the condition and progress of Hawaiians. It also was interested in other Polynesian groups. Mr. Bishop was a Founder of this society and served as its President.

Hawaiian Immigration Society

The Hawaiian Immigration Society aided in bringing workers and people into Hawai'i. Mr. Bishop served on the Executive Committee.

Honolulu Chamber of Commerce

The Honolulu Chamber of Commerce was interested in the solid economic good of Hawai'i. Mr. Bishop served as President for eight years.

The Social Science Association of Honolulu

The Social Science Association of Honolulu discussed topics about the general well-being of people. Members were intelligent community leaders. Mr. Bishop was a member from 1886 through 1892.

Photo by Williams, courtesy of Bishop Museum

Mr. Bishop served in many ways.

Other Interests

Mr. Bishop took great interest in horses. He loved horseback riding. The horses served him well. In return Mr. Bishop saw that they were cared for properly. He was kind to animals. He suggested that a horse named *"Grant"* retire in comfort. The old horse had been faithful. Mr. Bishop wrote, *"Were I at hand I would give him some oats and sugar, or a 'mash', which might suit the condition of his teeth better."*

Additional interests drew Mr. Bishop's attention. These included the Pacific Cable, the Telephone and the Electric Light, and Oʻahu Railway and Land Company.

In all these community and other interests Mr. Bishop served well. He gave his best to everything he did.

Live to Give

Mr. Bishop served to develop Hawai'i's resources and wealth. He used all his skills and gifts to help others. From what he developed he kept nothing for himself. He returned it all to Hawai'i. He gave to churches, schools and hospitals. He gave to institutions of science and of mercy. He gave to worthy and needy individuals. He benefited many people. He lived to give. Mr. Bishop's extent of giving is shown by the list of his beneficiaries.

1. Alumni Association of the Kamehameha Schools
2. American Board of Commissioners for Foreign Missions
3. American Relief Fund
4. Bernice Pauahi Bishop Museum
5. Board of the Hawaiian Evangelical Association
6. Celebration of "Founder's Day" at The Kamehameha Schools
7. Central Union Church
8. Children's Playgrounds in Honolulu
9. Free Kindergartens in Honolulu
10. Hampton Normal and Agricultural Institute
11. Hawaiian Historical Society and The Polynesian Society of New Zealand

12. Hilo Boys' Boarding School

13. Honolulu Library and Reading Room Association

14. Ka'iulani Home for Young Women in Honolulu

15. The Kamehameha Schools

    - Scholarships

    - Salary of the Chaplain

    - Construction of Bishop Hall at the School for Boys

    - Construction of the Preparatory Department

    - Construction of part of the School for Girls

    - Bernice Pauahi Bishop Memorial Chapel

16. Kapi'olani Maternity Home in Honolulu

17. Kaumakapili Church

18. Kawaiaha'o Church

19. Kohala Girls' School

20. Makawao Female Seminary

21. Mauna'ala (Royal Mausoleum)

22. Mauna'olu Seminary

23. Mid-Pacific Institute

24. Night Schools in Honolulu

25. Public Education in Hawai'i

26. Punahou School (O'ahu College)

27. Queen's Hospital

28. Waialua Female Seminary

29. Young Men's Christian Association

30. Many individuals either named or anonymous (not named)

Mr. Bishop set up a trust to see to his wishes. It is called the Charles Reed Bishop Trust, dated August 1, 1895.

Leaving Hawai‘i

Hawai‘i was Mr. Bishop's home for forty-eight years. Hawai‘i was where he had spent most of his life. He became a citizen of Hawai‘i. He married and worked in Hawai‘i where he was successful and highly respected. He was loved by all. Hawai‘i was a vital part of him. He was a vital part of Hawai‘i.

But the day came when Mr. Bishop would say goodbye to Hawai‘i. He would leave the land he had come to love. On March 2, 1894, Mr. Bishop boarded the ship Australia and sailed to San Francisco. He was seventy-two years of age.

Mr. Bishop left Hawai'i on the ship Australia.

Why did Mr. Bishop leave Hawai'i? One could say he left for personal reasons or even for political reasons. Perhaps the fall of the monarchy had discouraged him. Maybe he left because Lili'uokalani and later the new Provisional Government did not give Princess Ka'iulani a chance to reign as Queen. One could say he left for new business opportunities or a cooler climate. But all this would be speculating, or guessing. What was Mr. Bishop's reason for leaving Hawai'i? His heart alone held the answer.

Now Mr. Bishop would live in a new place. He would live in California.

Mr. Bishop would live in California.

Part Three

LIFE IN CALIFORNIA

Later Years

1894 - 1915

Settling in California

Mr. Bishop arrived in the city of San Francisco aboard the ship Australia. He moved into an apartment in the Occidental Hotel. The apartment became his new home. It also became a place of hospitality. Mr. Bishop welcomed visitors who were on their way to Hawai'i or who had come from Hawai'i.

Work and Interests

As he had always done, Mr. Bishop worked hard. He never slowed down. He was Vice President as well as a Director of the Bank of California. His main responsibility was to manage the internal affairs of the bank. His attendance record at directors' meetings was perfect. In fact, his last meeting was just two weeks before he died. Mr. Bishop was busy to the very end.

Mr. Bishop was always concerned about helping people in need. The Right Reverend Henry Bond Restarick shared a story about receiving such help. At that time he was the Bishop of the American Episcopal Church in Honolulu. He had sailed from Honolulu to San Francisco. Bishop Restarick was very troubled about a serious problem. He needed expert advice. He went to Mr. Bishop's home in San Francisco at eight o'clock one night. He told Mr. Bishop his trouble.

Mr. Bishop listened carefully. He showed deep, sympathetic concern. Then he exclaimed, *"I know the person you must see."* He called the person by telephone and found him at home. Mr. Bishop assured his visitor, *"I will go with you."*

Bishop Restarick protested because the night was cold and damp. Although Mr. Bishop was eighty-two years old, he insisted on going with Bishop Restarick. They walked down the stairs of the Occidental Hotel. Mr. Bishop never took the elevator. They rode a street car to the friend's home.

Mr. Bishop's friend was very helpful. He gave valuable advice to solve the problem. Mr. Bishop offered Bishop Restarick monetary help. But he declined Mr. Bishop's offer. Mr. Bishop had given him more than money. He had given him sympathetic friendship and personal help. For that Bishop Restarick would always be grateful.

Photo courtesy of Bishop Museum

Mr. Bishop at age 84.

San Francisco Earthquake

On April 18, 1906, a strong earthquake rocked San Francisco. It started a deadly fire and caused a lot of damage. Mr. Bishop was eighty-four years old. He remained calm and quickly left the hotel. He hired a driver and wagon. They drove away to safety.

Mr. Bishop lost some very valuable papers in the earthquake and fire. He had kept his wife's pictures, papers and all of her letters in his apartment. He had intended to put them in a safe place like the Bishop Museum. But they were destroyed before he could send them to the Museum. His copy books were also destroyed. These contained his many letters. What an unfortunate loss for historians and writers!

Mr. Bishop resettled in Berkeley. From there he wrote to his friends in Hawai'i. He assured them of his safety. In part he wrote:

> *"The sight of so much of ruin and want is distressing. We who have comfortable lodgings and are safe have great reason to be thankful."*

Counselor, Advisor, Friend

Throughout his years in California, Mr. Bishop kept in touch with his friends in Hawai'i. Mr. Bishop counseled and advised various individuals. He did this largely through the writing of letters. Not only was he a counselor and advisor, he was also a true friend.

One of Mr. Bishop's friends was Arthur C. Alexander. In a speech about Mr. Bishop he noted:

> "He [Mr. Bishop] was a wise counselor and guide, who never shirked any task however hard and disagreeable."

> "...I called on him [Mr. Bishop] on several occasions in his simply furnished quarters in the Occidental Hotel of San Francisco, and always came away with a warm feeling in my heart. He appeared apparently cold and unemotional to strangers, but it was only skin deep."

Ninetieth Birthday

On January 25, 1912, friends of Mr. Bishop gathered in Honolulu to celebrate his ninetieth birthday. They met at the Roof Garden of the Alexander Young Hotel. A large number of people came. Present were the Governor and Chief Justice. Also attending were representatives from educational, charitable and religious institutions. They came from The Kamehameha Schools, Punahou School, Mid-Pacific Institute, The Board of Education, Hawaiian Board of Missions, and Catholic Mission. There were also representatives from the Chamber of Commerce and Merchants' Association.

Photo courtesy of Bishop Museum

Mr. Bishop (center) with relatives in California.

Mr. Bishop was not present. But his friends wanted very much to pay him tribute. They held him in high esteem. They wished to speak of his upright character. They wanted to express their great admiration for Mr. Bishop. Their words were published in a booklet and sent to Mr. Bishop. In this way they honored him.

Mr. Bishop deeply appreciated the tribute from his friends. He wrote them a letter of gratitude. He closed with these words:

> *"To all who have congratulated me on my birthday I wish to express heartfelt thanks and to wish that the remaining years of their lives may be as many as they desire and are filled with God's choicest blessings."*

Death of a Hero

Three years later, at the age of ninety-three, Mr. Bishop died. He died in Berkeley on June 7, 1915. News of his death reached Hawaiʻi quickly. It saddened everyone. Flags were immediately lowered to half staff. The Capitol, Judiciary Building, and City Hall lowered their flags. Banks and businesses lowered their flags. All schools, both public and private, lowered their flags. This gesture showed the great respect people of all Hawaiʻi had for Mr. Bishop.

Upon hearing the news of Mr. Bishop's death, Queen Liliʻuokalani grieved. She felt deeply the loss of a lifelong friend. She shared these words:

> *"In common with those who have known Mr. Bishop for a life time, I feel the news of his death most keenly, and can truly say that his loss to Hawaiʻi and the Hawaiians is irreparable."*

Royal Ceremony

The ashes of Mr. Bishop arrived from San Francisco in a metal urn on June 22, 1915. They were brought to Honolulu by Wallace Alexander, a friend, on the steamship Matsonia. The urn was taken immediately to Kawaiahaʻo Church. There up front in the sanctuary a stand was covered with a black velvet cloth. Upon the cloth was laid a beautiful ʻilima lei. The urn was put in a mahogany case and placed upon the stand. White lilies surrounded the stand.

    Mr. Bishop was given the ceremony reserved only for Hawaiian royalty. The waving of kāhili, or royal standards, took place. The old name chants of the Kamehameha family were chanted. The vigil, or watch, continued throughout the night. Thousands of people came to pay their respects.

Photo by L.E. Edgeworth, courtesy of Bishop Museum

The urn with Mr. Bishop's ashes was brought to Honolulu on the steamship Matsonia.

The ceremony for Mr. Bishop was a rare event. It honored a Caucasian man, a man who was not of Hawaiian ancestry. Only one other time had this happened. It was at the death of John Young, the trusted Caucasian friend and advisor of Kamehameha the Great. Now eighty years later Mr. Bishop was so honored.

The funeral service was held the next day, June 23. Beautiful flowers and fragrant lei formed a backdrop in the Church. They were given by lifelong friends, by fellow workers, by beneficiaries of his generosity and service. A beautiful wreath of orchids was given by Queen Liliʻuokalani.

Hundreds of citizens, both men and women, filled the Church. Besides the Queen there were many community leaders. They represented churches, businesses, education, government and the armed forces. All had come to honor the memory of Hawaiʻi's beloved citizen and great benefactor.

Photo courtesy of Bishop Museum

Kawaiahaʻo Church where the funeral service for Mr. Bishop was held.

The Queen took her seat. The honorary pall bearers entered. A quartet sang the hymn "*Still, Still With Thee*." One member of the quartet was from The Kamehameha Schools. Another member was from Punahou. Their voices blended in harmony. The Scripture was read.

   Then the Reverend Henry Hodges Parker, Pastor of Kawaiahaʻo Church, spoke. He had known Mr. Bishop as someone who was loved by people all over Hawaiʻi. The Pastor said that he knew no man more upright, straightforward and honest than Mr. Bishop.

The Reverend Parker spoke these words:

"There was no fuss, no sham, no double dealing about him. His word could always be depended upon. Upright, square and fearless, he was a man in his every word and action. He was always loyal to right; he never believed in doing wrong that right might come of it.

"The royal Hawaiian motto, 'Ua mau ke ea o ka 'aina i ka pono,' 'the life of the land is established in righteousness,' was no mere sentiment with Mr. Bishop. He believed in it and in his everyday life carried out its injunction. Mr. Bishop was human; he was humane. He was always sober and serious. His austere appearance gave one the idea that he was entirely unapproachable. This was not so; he was most approachable, in fact.

"I cannot say that he is dead. He is only away. His spirit is here. The work for good that he did in life will abide with us. As a philanthropist, I have known none greater than he."

The Reverend Parker closed his message with a prayer. He was followed by the Reverend Henry Keli'ikuniaupuni Poepoe, Pastor of Kaumakapili Church, who gave an address in Hawaiian. He talked about the good Mr. Bishop had done during his lifetime. Now this good will endure to benefit the human race.

Then the quartet sang *"Peace, Perfect Peace."* The Reverend Parker pronounced a short benediction.

At Rest with Pauahi

When the church service ended, a pallbearer, Fred W. Beckley, carried the urn to a waiting automobile. He was followed by the many people who had come to mourn the passing of Mr. Bishop. The solemn procession moved slowly on its way to Mauna'ala, the Royal Mausoleum, in Nu'uanu Valley.

The ceremony at the Kamehameha crypt was short and simple. This crypt, or underground vault, was the burial site of members of the Kamehameha family. Mr. Bishop's cousin, Eben Faxon Bishop, carried the urn into the crypt. He placed it **near** Mrs. Bishop's casket. Then Prince Jonah Kūhiō Kalaniana'ole, of royal descent, placed the urn **on** Mrs. Bishop's casket. The Reverend Parker spoke a short benediction. Everyone then walked up the stairs and out of the crypt.

Monument marking the location of the Kamehameha crypt.

Before Mr. Bishop's burial it was possible to go down the stairs into the Kamehameha crypt. But now with Mr. Bishop laid to rest with his beloved Pauahi, the crypt would be closed permanently. The heavy metal doors were shut and bolted. Later a special tombstone was erected nearby in loving memory of Charles Reed Bishop.

The Charles Reed Bishop tombstone.

Greatest Benefactor

Seven weeks after the burial of Mr. Bishop, a beautiful tribute was shared in writing. On August 12, 1915, the Trustees of the Charles Reed Bishop Trust wrote:

> *"He was Hawai'i's greatest benefactor, and because of the carefully planned form of his charities his influence does not cease with his death. As long as civilization exists on these western shores so long will men and women, particularly those of the younger years, arise to bear testimony to the helping hand, and uplifting spirit of Charles R. Bishop."*

Charles Reed Bishop possessed the heart of a hero.

Conclusion

A hero is an ordinary person who responds to challenging situations in extraordinary ways. He goes far beyond the ordinary way. He sets noble goals. He dreams big dreams and reaches for the stars. He commits himself to worthy tasks. He endures and perseveres. He inspires others and serves them as well. Charles Reed Bishop was such a person. He is a shining example of a true hero.

Mr. Bishop lived a life that spanned ninety-three years. While growing up in New York he learned early the value of building a noble character. In Hawai'i he expanded his many skills and applied them in creative ways. He married Princess Bernice Pauahi whom he loved deeply. During his later years in California he continued to use his talents wisely.

Charles Reed Bishop possessed the heart of a hero. That heart was a heart of love, integrity and truth. It revealed wisdom, loyalty and trust. It showed kindness, humility and respect. It demonstrated friendship, generosity and service. It proved to be a heart of courage, compassion and dedication.

Charles Reed Bishop the person is gone now. But the precious legacy, or gift he left behind, lives on. That legacy is his life of honorable deeds and worthy achievements.

Charles Reed Bishop continues to serve as a fine role model for others to follow. Listen to his words of wisdom and take heed: *"So long as we are in the right, we may reasonably trust in God for His help; let us always try to be in the right."*

Bibliography

Books and Pamphlets

Akana, Akaiko. *Light Upon the Mist. A Reflection of Wisdom for the Future Generations of Native Hawaiians*. Kailua-Kona, Hawai'i: Mahina Productions, 1992.

Aspects of Hawaiian Life and Environment. Honolulu: Kamehameha Schools Press, 1971.

Black, Cobey and Kathleen Dickenson Mellen. *Princess Pauahi Bishop and Her Legacy*. Honolulu: The Kamehameha Schools Press, 1965.

The Bridge: Glens Falls History Suggested by Four Bridges Spanning the Hudson River. Glens Falls, New York: First National Bank of Glens Falls, 19--.

Charles Reed Bishop - Hawai'i 1846-1894 - January 25, 1972 Sesquicentennial. Honolulu, Hawai'i: Office of Library Services, Department of Education, 1972.

Curtis, Caroline. *Bits of Biography*. Honolulu: Kamehameha Schools Preparatory Department, 19--.

- - -. *Builders of Hawai'i*. Honolulu: The Kamehameha Schools Press, 1966.

Kanahele, George Hu'eu Sanford. *Pauahi: The Kamehameha Legacy*. Honolulu: Kamehameha Schools Press, 1986.

Kent, Harold Winfield. *An Album of Likenesses*. Honolulu: Bernice Pauahi Bishop Museum, 1972.

- - -. *Charles Reed Bishop: Man of Hawai'i.* Palo Alto, California: Pacific Books Publishers, 1965.

- - -, comp. and ed. *Charles Reed Bishop: Letter File*. Honolulu: Alexander & Baldwin, et. al., 1972.

Krout, Mary H. *The Memoirs of Hon. Bernice Pauahi Bishop*. New York: The Knickerbocker Press, 1908.

Mitchell, Donald D. Kilolani. *Kū Kilakila 'O Kamehameha. A Historical Account of the Campuses of the Kamehameha Schools.* Honolulu: Kamehameha Schools/Bernice Pauahi Bishop Estate, 1993.

Nellist, George Ferguson Mitchell, ed. *The Story of Hawai'i and Its Builders.* Honolulu: Honolulu Star-Bulletin, Ltd., 1925.

Richards, Mary Atherton. *The Chiefs' Children's School.* Honolulu: Honolulu Star-Bulletin, Ltd., 1937.

Scott, M.M., et al. *Tribute to Charles R. Bishop, January 25, 1912.* Honolulu: Friends of Mr. Bishop, 1912.

Williams, Julie Stewart. *Princess Bernice Pauahi Bishop.* Honolulu: Kamehameha Schools/ Bernice Pauahi Bishop Estate, 1992.

Wills and Deeds of Trust: Bernice P. Bishop Estate, Bernice P. Bishop Museum, Charles R. Bishop Estate. 3rd ed. Honolulu: Printshop of Hawai'i Co., Ltd., 1957.

Periodicals and Other Sources

Alexander, Arthur C. "Charles R. Bishop, as Remembered by Arthur C. Alexander." ts. Archives, Midkiff Learning Center, Kamehameha Schools, Honolulu.

Apple, Russ. "Tales of Old Hawai'i - Charles Bishop: the Man Who Created an Estate." *Honolulu Star-Bulletin* 4 Nov. 1985: A-13.

Apple, Russ and Peg. "Faithful Friend of Royalty." *Honolulu Star-Bulletin* 22 Jan. 1972: A-10.

"Birthday Benefactor Celebrated by Punahou." *Pacific Commercial Advertiser* 26 Jan. 1915: 5.

Bishop, Charles Reed. Address. Founder's Day. Kamehameha Schools, Honolulu. 19 Dec. 1887.

- - -. "An Inside View of the Reign of Lunalilo." *Hawaiian Historical Society Annual Report* 49 (1940): 12-28.

- - -. "The Purpose of the School." *Handicraft* Jan., 1889: 1,3.

- - -. "To Rev. C.M. Hyde, D.D." 11 Feb. 1897. Letter in *Bishop Museum Letters Book 1*. Honolulu: Bishop Museum, 19--.

- - -. "To S.M. Damon." 20 Feb. 1901. Letter in *Kamehameha Schools Letters Book 4*. Honolulu: Kamehameha Schools, 19--.

- - -. "To S.M. Damon." 9 Oct. 1911. Letter in *Kamehameha Schools Letters Book 11*. Honolulu: Kamehameha Schools, 19--.

- - -. "To the Trustees." 6 Apr. 1910. Letter in *Kamehameha Schools Letters Book 10*. Honolulu: Kamehameha Schools, 19--.

"Bishop Hall Dedication Punahou School." A Program for the Dedication of Bishop Hall, Punahou School, April 23, 1972.

Brigham, William T. "Charles Reed Bishop, 1822-1915." *Thrum's Annual* (1916): 63-71.

"A Century of Service to Hawai'i." *Honolulu Star-Bulletin* 14 Aug. 1958: 6.

"Charles R. Bishop, friend of Hawai'i, dead; was greatest philanthropist Hawai'i ever knew." *Pacific Commercial Advertiser* 8 June 1915: 9,12.

"Charles R. Bishop—Philanthropist." *The Friend* July 1915: 156-157.

"Charles Reed Bishop." *The Friend* July 1915: 148.

"Charles Reed Bishop." *The Friend* June 1948: 12-13.

Clarke, Mariajane. "Charles R. Bishop." *Paradise of the Pacific / Holiday Edition* Dec. 1948: 75-78, 125.

"Cremation In San Francisco Present Plan." *Honolulu Star-Bulletin* 9 June 1915: 2.

Cummings, Margaret Kamm. "Hawai'i's Mr. Bishop." *Honolulu Star-Bulletin - Hawaiian Life* 17 Dec. 1955: 4.

Damon, Ethel M. and Josephine Sullivan. "A Historical View of The Kamehameha Schools - Prepared for the Fortieth Anniversary at the Request of President Frank E. Midkiff." *The Friend* Dec. 1928: 267-314.

"Editorial Notes." *Handicraft* Jan. 1892: 2-3.

"Fact Sheet: Life of Charles Reed Bishop for Use in the Commemoration of the Sesquicentennial of Charles Reed Bishop's birth..." ts. Hawaiian Studies, Midkiff Learning Center, Kamehameha Schools, Honolulu.

"Founder's Day." *Handicraft* Jan. 1889: 2.

Frankel, Chuck. "The Story of a Young Man Who Fulfilled His Dreams." *Honolulu Star-Bulletin* 5 May 1965: C8.

"Funeral of Late Charles Reed Bishop Attended by Royalty and High Officials." *The Pacific Commercial Advertiser* 24 June 1915: 3.

"Funeral Rites Over Remains of C.R. Bishop [in San Francisco, June 9, 1915]" *Honolulu Star-Bulletin* 10 June 1915: 9.

"Hawai'i Loses Good Friend in C.R. Bishop." *Honolulu Star-Bulletin* 8 June 1915: 6.

Hickok, Peggy. "Punahou Reopens Hall Named for Great Benefactor." *Honolulu Star-Bulletin* 4 Jan. 1951: 9.

Joesting, Edward. "Hawai'i's Pioneer Banker." *The Saturday Star-Bulletin* 16 Aug. 1958: 6-7.

Johnson, Hal. "A Story About Charles Reed Bishop." *The Saturday Star-Bulletin* 15 Jan. 1955: 4.

Jones, Mrs. Pierre. "Bernice Pauahi Bishop." Address. Founder's Day Celebration. Kamehameha Schools, Honolulu. 19 Dec. 1923.

"Kamehameha Preparatory School." *Handicraft* Jan. 1889: 4.

Kent, Harold W. "Charles Reed Bishop." Address. 72nd Convocation of The Kamehameha Schools. Honolulu, Hawai'i. 7 Sept. 1958.

- - -. "Charles R. Bishop: Cleverness and Compassion." *The Sunday Star-Bulletin & Advertiser* 21 November 1971: D6.

- - -, comp. "Charles Reed Bishop Genealogy." ts. Hawaiian Studies, Midkiff Learning Center, Kamehameha Schools, Honolulu.

- - -. "Three Column Table: Portraits of Charles Reed and Bernice Pauahi Bishop." ts. Hawaiian Studies, Midkiff Learning Center, Kamehameha Schools, Honolulu.

"The Legacy of Charles Reed Bishop." *Economic Indicators* [Research Department, First Hawaiian Bank] July/August 1983: 1.

"Many Tributes Paid to Services of C.R. Bishop to Hawaiʻi." *Honolulu Star-Bulletin* 8 June 1915: 7.

"The Meiji Mystery - Bishop Bank Discovers Rare Document in Old Trunk." *Honolulu Star-Bulletin* 20 Dec. 1959: 8.

"Memorial Service Revives Royal Custom." *The Friend* July 1915: 157.

Midkiff, Frank E. Address. Commemorating the 100th Anniversary of Charles Reed Bishop's Arrival in Hawaiʻi. Kamehameha Schools, Honolulu. 12 Oct. 1946.

"Obituary." *The Friend* July 1915: 148.

"1822 - Charles Reed Bishop - 1915." *Paradise of the Pacific* June 1915: 14-15.

"Punahou Students Pay Tribute to Memory of Charles R. Bishop." *The Pacific Commercial Advertiser* 10 June 1915: 9.

Restarick, H.B. "Charles R. Bishop Opened Honolulu's First Bank and Advised Five Rulers." *Honolulu Star-Bulletin* 8 Aug. 1931: 6.

"Royal Honors Given Ashes of Mr. Bishop." *The Pacific Commercial Advertiser* 23 June 1915: 7,9.

"Silent Throngs Pay Respects to Late C.R. Bishop." *Honolulu Star-Bulletin* 23 June 1915: 1,3.

Smith, Jared G. "Concerning Charles R. Bishop." *Honolulu Advertiser* 31 Mar. 1957: A10.

Smith, Walter Gifford. "The Banker and the Princess." *The Mid-Pacific Magazine* Dec. 1915: 581-587.

"A Story About Charles Reed Bishop." *Honolulu Star-Bulletin* 15 Jan. 1955: 4.

"Take Ashes of Late C.R. Bishop to Kawaiahaʻo." *Honolulu Star-Bulletin* 16 June 1915: 1.

"The Turrill Collection." [Letters written by Charles Reed Bishop] *Hawaiian Historical Society Annual Report* 66 (1957): 26-92.

About the Author

    Peter Galuteria was born and raised in the Kakaʻako district of Honolulu, Hawaiʻi. He attended Pohukaina Elementary School, Washington Intermediate School and McKinley High School. He earned a B.A. degree from Houghton College in New York; M.R.E. from Fuller Theological Seminary in Pasadena, California; M.Ed. from the University of Southern California; and M.L.S. from the University of Hawaiʻi.

    For nearly thirty years Mr. Galuteria taught at Kamehameha Schools. He served as the Christian Education instructor for grades kindergarten through eight, a classroom teacher in grades four and five of the Elementary School, the librarian in the Learning Center for grades seven and eight, and a reading teacher in the Kamehameha Schools Intermediate Reading Program of the Community Education Division. He retired in 1989.

    Peter authored the book *Lunalilo*, published by Kamehameha Schools Bishop Estate in 1993. It had long been his desire also to write a book about Charles Reed Bishop, founder of Kamehameha's Preparatory Department. As a teacher and librarian, he was very cognizant of the need for a biography of Mr. Bishop appropriate especially for students in grades five through eight. His goal has been achieved in *Heart of a Hero: Charles Reed Bishop*.